What People are Saying about

Shelters by Jesus
PART TWO

If you have studied Systematic Theology and memorized Bible verses but still struggle with believing, this is the book for you. If you do not even know what a Systematic Theology is but are wondering if God is real, this is the book for you. If you believe God is real but doubt whether He is alive and well and still performing miracles, this is the book for you. It is a simple, easy to read book by a country pastor with a child-like faith that has opened the door to miracles too numerous to count. You will finish the book in a few hours, but the impact will be life-changing.

—*Paul Michalsk*
President, NCS New
Canaan (founding Chapter of the New Canaan Society).

Perhaps it would be too harsh to say that the Church, here in America, appears to have become so dependent upon it's structure and standards of organization to ever consider a ministry like what is happening in Skowhegan at the Trinity Evangelical Free Church, and Shelter by Jesus without first forming a committee and acquiring a budget. Yet, the testimonies in this book paint a clear picture of God's continuing work and blessing in and upon a ministry that does just that. It's as if Jesus is calling out to the church just as He did with the apostle Peter, to step out of the boat and do what would normally be called impossible. It would appear that faith and trust in God is all that is required to build homeless shelters, feed the hungry, clothe the poor, and win souls to Christ. Imagine.

—*Peter J. Bolduc*

The book you have before you documents the work of a simple servant of God, who consistently makes courageous choices to love the lost and hurting, in the name of Christ. As a minister, I know that Richard holds a decision-making scale in his hands.... we all do. On one side of the scale are heavy questions like, "Is it safe to house homeless people; how much would it cost; what about critics, the town or the neighbors; what about liability; and what if giving plummets?" On the other side of Richard's scale are the words of Christ that say "Love your neighbor"...and since He puts such weight in the words of his "Dad"...the scale tips every time toward Jesus. This book contains vibrant illustrations of the life of a disciple of Christ Jesus; a life and a passion that he shares equally with his dear and courageous wife Selma.

—*Rev. David A. Johnson*
Sr. Pastor, Grace Church, East Dennis, MA

November 27, 2016

In case you don't read any further, I highly recommend this book and to follow the example of Faith that pastor Berry sets forth inside these covers. On May 25 2016 I attended a NH Pastors Alliance gathering in Pembroke NH to meet and hear from Pastor Jim Cymbala from Brooklyn Tabernacle. GOD in his providence knew that there was going to be someone else there that I needed to meet. As I stood waiting in the hallway for two of my Christian brothers to return, Pastor Berry approached me, introduced himself, and told me he wanted to bless me with a copy of his book, *Sheltered by Jesus.* That was the beginning of what has developed quite quickly into an awesome relationship. He has visited and has spoken at our Church and my wife and I have been to the shelter now on two different occasions. The latest being just a few days ago to help Amy and Tim in the kitchen with Thanksgiving Dinner. This second book, just as in the first book, is a chronicle of GOD'S mighty power, providence and promise to fulfill the needs of those whom he has called into ministry. There is absolutely no true calling of the LORD that he will not provide all things necessary to fulfill the calling. Albeit somewhat subtle Pastor Berry is calling for the Church of Jesus Christ to awaken and stop living in shallow faith and to walk in the fullness of God's promises. We are no longer citizens of this place but of the household of God. However, he has left us here to be the hands and feet of JESUS as there is much to do before he returns. Through the gifts of the Holy Spirit each one of us has been given an inexhaustible supply of "spiritual currency" that GOD expects us to spend daily for the building up and edification of the body and the advancement of His Kingdom. I am encouraged to see that Pastor Berry has caught the vision and is working tirelessly for the advancement of God's Kingdom. I am Looking forward to serving with and along side of Pastor Berry in the future as much as the LORD wills.

—Jeffrey L. Winn
"Spirit Revolution Outreach Ministry" and Prison Ministry Leader @ CROSSROADS CHURCH of Littleton, NH

Richard Berry, the hick from Skowhegan, Maine with Dad guiding his pen has written again a book so moving to make you laugh and cry and you can't put it down. Hopefully as you read this book you will realize how precious each person is to the Lord and should be to us as well whether they are from the outhouse or the penthouse.

—Ron & Faye Brewer

Isn't that just like God? He says He will do more than provide for His people, He will give an abundance. Pastor Berry brings his homeless to God in a spirit of Love, obedience and sacrifice, no matter how insignificant they may think they are. Expecting God to do far beyond what can be imagined and trusting God to meet the needs of His children, He wants to lavish His children with spiritual blessings, even to overflowing.

The spiritual gift of miracles is one of the spiritual gifts listed in 1 Corinthians 12:10 where the NIV calls it "miraculous power." We absolutely believe that God still heals and works miracles today. Pastor Berry shows us time and time again, the lesson is to walk in fellowship with the Lord and obey Him, we will be open to His will. And when we are in God's will, He fulfills our needs, and His mercy to us never runs short. Praise God! Pastor Berry teaches us how to find victory and reward by encouraging each of us to reach out and fulfill our call in compassion ministry. Compelling! Riveting! A must to have in every library!

—Deb and Bruce Wilkins

Like a cozy blanket on a winter night or a cool drink on a summer day, this collection of stories will warm your heart and refresh your spirit.

—Rev. J.H. "Jake" and Barbary Neubauer

"Pastor Berry offers a sequel to his first book, Sheltered by Jesus, filled with anecdotes that are as down to earth as they are theologically sophisticated and convicting, reinforcing the reality that each of us can be engaged in the process of connecting the virtues of divinity with the needs of humanity, if we are willing. Our family (with high school and college teens) read a chapter at dinner every night. Pastor Berry's homespun narratives became true-to-life parables for valuable conversation that eventually lead us to spend family time at the shelter in Skowhegan, and we will be back. Read it, if you dare."

— Dave Rucquoi,
Elder, Hope Evangelical Free Church, Wilton, CT

I have read the manuscript for this new book and am very moved once more. I was moved to faith by the first one and am moved to action by book 2. This is a different book than book one, but it is a great challenge to not just feel FOR the homeless, but to reach out and "feel" the homeless.

I am excited to have the book on my hands and read it through and as you do the same I trust you will ask "What can I do?" And then I pray you will look to Father and say "Here am I send me."

The greatest testament to this book will be when people like you and I commit to help that one person who is in front of us, not judging their need but meeting it.

—Pastor Steve Nute

One Saturday I went to our ministry mailbox and when I opened it there was an unexpected package. This package was from a gentleman I have never met before and contained a book written by Pastor Berry about his homeless ministry in Maine. The man who sent it to me said he saw a post on Facebook about our ministry to the homeless and thought the book would be an encouragement. Our ministry has been working hard to get donations to help the poor and homeless in our area. We were praying daily for provision from God to continue our efforts. I went to the ministry mailbox expecting monetary provision but instead I got, a book...

I was upset that there were no checks, no money, and no provision, just a book. I tried to be positive and thank God for the book and the fact that someone thought enough of me to send it. I even told myself that the book was about another homeless ministry and that I may learn a few things to apply to this ministry. However, as I looked at the book, I still thought to myself "God where are you when this ministry and the people we serve need you?!"

Like any "good" ministry leader I tossed the book on the counter, ignored it and stewed over the lack of funds in the ministry account. The next day, I went to church as usual, did my best to worship and then went out to feed and love on the homeless people we serve every week. I was putting up a front; in all honesty I was discouraged. When I got home and saw the book sitting there, something in me told me to read the Foreword. You need to understand I NEVER read the Foreword of a book, EVER. But that day I did. I read about a man who had been praying for money to keep his ministry afloat and instead got a CD in the mail with a message from Pastor Berry. It was an instant realization that God had done it again. Of course He did!

I read the book cover to cover that night and was so moved to hear of the amazing things that God had done in Pastor Berry's ministry and the real difference it was making in Maine. I was at a place where I had lost all hope that God would help our ministry and that it would eventually just fade away. However, this book provided the encouragement I needed. It reinforced that God still does miracles today. He is the Great I AM, not the Great I WAS. I was encouraged that God can use the simplest of men (that includes me for sure) to bring Him the most glory and touch many lives in the process.

I knew I that I had to call Pastor Berry the next day. He greeted me by saying "I have been waiting for your call". God did it again! Not only did Pastor Berry take my call but also spent time on the phone with me discussing my ministry. He even prayed to Dad for both the ministry and my own needs. Then he called Pastor Cortese, the man who wrote the Foreword, and he called me too. This was another layer of encouragement, which I desperately needed. I do not claim to know what God is doing with our ministry, but thanks to Pastor Berry writing this book and Pastor Cortese writing the Foreword I realize that I do not need to know all the details. I just need to trust God, enjoy the ride, lift my hands in prayer and see what God can do. I was expecting to get a check in the mail, but that didn't happen. Then I expected to read this book and gain a few nuggets of insight to apply to our ministry, but what I received was much more precious and beyond monetary worth-hope, encouragement, renewed faith and new friends in Christ.

Let God use this book to inspire you to serve and trust Him too. After all, we all live Sheltered by Jesus.

—*Bob Gardner*

Executive Director Messengers of Hope Mission, Inc. Odessa, FL

Shelters by Jesus
PART TWO

SHELTERS by Jesus

PART TWO

The Story Continues

RICHARD BERRY

Shelters By Jesus
PART TWO
The Story Continues

All stories detailed herein are factual; however, certain names of individuals and companies have been omitted or reduced in order to protect the identity of these persons or companies.

ISBN: 978-0-911802-19-1

Published in the United States of America
Published by
NextStep Resources
7890 12th Ave South Minneapolis, MN 55425
(800) 444-2665
Design, Layout and Format: Kim Gardell, Graphic Design

Proceeds from the sale of this book go to support the ministry of the Skowhegan Homeless Shelter

TABLE OF CONTENTS

DEDICATION

I would like to dedicate this book to my wife, Selma (Merry) Berry. She has always been there, encouraging me to try to do things I did not believe I was capable of doing. She has had more faith in me than I've had in myself. Jesus used her to inspire me to step out and attempt what I believed was the impossible. In my opinion, the toughest job in the world is to be a pastor's wife. They suffer silently when their husband is crying behind closed doors. Without her and Jesus, none of this would have been possible. The Lord gave Eve to Adam because He knew she was what he needed. He gave Selma to me for the exact same reason, only she did not lead me astray, but instead kept me moving forward when I would have given up. I pray that all pastors would be blessed with a true helper as God has blessed me.

FOREWORD

My wife and I are truly humbled and honored to be a part of this book. It is a privilege to witness the continuing miracles from God through a homeless shelter in a small town in rural Maine. Since becoming the chairman of the board of this ministry this past year, Pastor Berry and I have grown extremely close. I can count the number of days on both hands that we have not spoken with or contacted each other. He and his wife have become dear friends of ours over this time. We laugh, cry, and sometimes just shrug our shoulders when things come up that challenge our faith. We have seen God weave our relationship together in such a way that only a mighty God such as ours could have done. What an amazing time we are in right now! Being in such close contact with Pastor Berry has not only allowed us to physically witness God's miracles for this shelter, but we have also experienced miracles and blessings in our own family, many of which have come to us through being a part of this ministry. Just as Pastor Berry went through a period of struggle before experiencing victories at the shelter, we also went through a period of having out faith tested before we saw the triumph of God's plan. As you read this book, and maybe read or re-read the first book, while the miracles being told are faith building and wonderful to read about, the struggles to get there are real, painful, and difficult to get through. Pastor Berry and all those involved in winning souls for Christ through this shelter need your prayers. Prayers for strength, guidance, and wisdom. It is truly an honor to be a part of this ministry and a part of Pastor Berry's life!

—Ken and Monica Allen

Owners, The Family Freeze Ice Cream Parlor in Wilton, Maine.

CHAPTER 1

YOU KNOW MY "Dad" is so amazing, but you would think the stories would have to come to an end sometime. He continues to amaze and confound me, however, and by now I'm sure you have come to the conclusion that, that is NOT ALL THAT DIFFICULT!!!

I find God using the craziest things to get His will done with this ministry. One day I was going to take my wife and my mom to the Amish store in Unity, Maine. Mom had never been there, but my wife and I had been there once and discovered the best doughnuts in the entire world (at least from my standpoint).

Before we left for the store, I did something that I rarely do. Now this may sound ridiculous to you, but I wore a hat. Not just any hat at that. It was a gift from Dwight, a former resident who wanted to do something special for everything the shelter had done for him. He shared how he didn't have much money, so he had this hat created special for me. It was quite ostentatious (big word that I asked my wife to spell for me). The hat had a cross, a bible, and "Man of Faith" across the front with "I Love Jesus" on the brim. I stuck out like a sore thumb just struck by a hammer! But the real reason I don't wear any hats as a rule, let alone one that would cause me to stand out like this "special one," is my hair. I have awesome hair for an old man. I do not want to cover it up, because from the hair line down I look like the Pillsbury Dough Boy on a bad day! So you strut what little you've got.

I walk into the store and as I am looking at the products on the shelves, a man behind the counter starts staring at me. His eyes followed me wherever I moved. Since I did not know anything about the Amish, I didn't know why he chose to stare at me. I mean, he couldn't see my hair because it was covered with this "special hat." Finally, he walked up to me and pointed toward the hat. Then he asked me, "Are you?" I brilliantly replied, "Am I What?" He said, "Are you a Man of Faith?" I replied, "I think so!" He then proceeded to ask me why I thought I was a Man of Faith. I began to share some of the stories of which I have been writing so far. That opened up a fantastic discussion where he proceeded to share his faith in Jesus. He told how he came to be a born again believer and had been baptized. He then went on to say, "We'd like to join you and help in any way we can at your shelter." He told how the Amish in that community had approached other shelters to offer their help. They were turned down because they wanted to pray with any resident to ask God to meet their needs. They were informed the shelters accepted state and federal funding, so praying was not allowed. He asked me if they could pray with our residents, and I excitedly proclaimed, "You can pray your little hearts out!" Since then, we now receive organic produce during harvesting season and my cooks go out of their minds over fresh veggies. We took down the barn we bought so we can put up the 48-bed family shelter where it was sitting, and the Amish showed up with a crew of 18 people of all ages and took almost all of the barn down in a day, while salvaging most of it so we could sell it. At the end of the day, a young 13-year old boy who had been working on a dead run all day came near to me. I said to him, "Son, I need to take a handful of Advil, because my back aches from watching you all day." I quickly learned that jokes were not their strong suit as he looked at me all serious and proclaimed, "Why? You haven't done a thing all day!" I lost it! I have just fallen in love with these God loving, hardworking and big hearted people. I later received a call from one of them who informed me how much the shelter had touched them. They took a homeless man into their home for the very first time, as they believed this is what God expected of them. I am totally blown away by what God can do with a hat that I do not wear! It was worth covering my hair so God could show off His Glory instead.

CHAPTER 2

I AM AMAZED and astonished how scriptures that I have read and taught for over 30 years are now coming to life in my ministry today. An example of that is found in 1 Kings Chapter 17 where the prophet Elijah is sent to a widow in Zarephath. Due to the disobedience of Israel, God has sent a drought and it is so bad that people are starving to death. Elijah is told to go to this widow and ask for food. She explains how she does not have enough to give to him. Actually, she is about to make a last meal for herself and her son and then they will die along with all the others. But, she then agrees to do it as God has commanded her and because of her willingness to feed Elijah in the face of starvation to herself and son, God does a miracle. Her food supply does not run out until the drought has ended. For me, this used to simply be a great story that I believed, but had very little to do with me and my ministry. That is until now, as it does apply to me today. The need of a miraculous and constant supply is necessary for this ministry to survive. One such miracle is the Amish joining us, but since we are now connected with the food bank, which is its own miracle, our food supplies have exploded! We now receive food from four supermarkets plus bakeries. We have now received supplies of dairy and deli that we never had before. We have needed to add more freezers and refrigerators and still can't hold it all. Last Christmas we were blessed to give away 1,500 pounds of meat out of our food pantry to families outside the shelter. We just recently gave away another 1,000 pounds of meat to families. I could never do justice to the looks on the faces of these people as they carry the food out to their vehicles. In 2015, we fed 80 to 100 residents a day plus an additional 700 households in 3 counties! I am not Elijah and I never met the widow of Zarephath, but this is not far from it. Jesus brought over 400 new converts to His kingdom this past year, and the miracles of showing compassion opened their hearts to Him.

There are so many stories that could be told of the impact caused through this food ministry. But one stands out in particular. I received a phone call from an elderly lady in town. She asked if we had any food at this time, and I shared that we did. She told me she was in great need but had no way to get to the shelter to pick it up. She did not have the five dollars to pay a taxi to get it for her. So I said, "I will deliver it to you personally." She was so excited I was coming that it was embarrassing. It was like the Pope was going to deliver a basket of food to a Catholic! I told my staff to really load me up so we could blow this lady away when I delivered the basket. It ended up with me getting blown away. When I arrived, I was greeted by this little old lady who was very tiny and very excited to see me. When I brought the food in, she grabbed me, hugged me, and began to cry so hard she was sobbing. She said, "Come with me so I can show you what you just did." She led me to her refrigerator and opened the freezer. It was empty. She then proceeded to open the refrigerator and it was as empty as the freezer. She continued to lead me by the hand to every cupboard door which she opened to show me. They were all empty as well. She did not have so much as a cracker in her house! She then said, "If you had not come today, I would not have had anything to eat!" Now she wasn't the only one crying. We shared a nice "ladies'" cry together! Usually I reserve my tears for behind closed doors, but this day caused the flood gates to open. It was as if "Dad" was saying to me, "This is your widow of Zarephath." The reason miracles do not seem to apply to the church today is because we fail to allow ourselves to be put in a situation that calls for a miracle. God is teaching me so many lessons as I continue to work with the homeless and the hungry.

CHAPTER 3

You know, sometimes God shows you the great need for ministry through someone else's eyes. I was privileged to meet a Jewish Rabbi the other day. My wife and I celebrated our 46th wedding anniversary and God used it to open up an opportunity to hear a story from this Rabbi. It had to be a "God thing" because of how it all came about. We were supposed to have breakfast at the resort at which we were staying, but overslept and had to hurry to catch a ship for a cruise. It ended up that we had more time than we thought so we decided to grab something at a small restaurant near where we were to board the ship. There was only this one couple eating there besides us. When I finished praying over our meal and said "Amen," the lady said "Amen" as well. She then proceeded to share how impressed she was to hear a prayer over the meal. She shared how she and her husband had just arrived in the area from Israel. As I shared that I was a pastor of a church with a homeless shelter, her husband Solomon told me he was a Rabbi. They were on a vacation to Nova Scotia so he didn't have on his Rabbi clothing, and his braids (I guess that's what they are called) were tucked under a baseball cap. We discussed compassion ministries, which was where their hearts were at. The discussion led to homelessness and they shared their view of what they had already seen in America where homelessness is concerned. They told me that when they got off their plane in Washington, D.C., they saw multitudes of homeless people on the streets. They were truly amazed and literally horrified to think America had such a disregard for their homeless in the richest nation in the world. Now you may argue the fact of us being the richest nation in the world, but that is how they viewed us. I was embarrassed! Not so much for our country as I was for our churches. I do not know how many churches there are in Washington, D.C., but they were invisible to this Rabbi and his wife as they surveyed a sight that made them sick to their stomachs.

I can relate to them somewhat from a past experience I had while adopting my son, Ricky, from San Salvador. As I walked down the streets of that city, I stepped over families lying on the sidewalk, many of whom were begging for food. It made me sick to my stomach as well. But, this was a third world country, not America! I kissed the ground when I arrived home with my new son in tow. I was proud that I could raise him in a country full with greater opportunities than he could have dreamed of if he remained in San Salvador. But, now some-one sees my country, full of churches proclaiming to serve my god, treating people as though they were invisible and not worth putting out an effort in the name of Jesus to meet their needs. God dealt with the

Apostle Peter in Acts Chapter 10 in a manner that would open his eyes to how God sees all people. Peter, being a Jew by birth, saw the Gentle as worthless, too unclean to be a part of any of their lives. Jesus showed him a vision to open his eyes to the truth that the Gentiles were as acceptable as any Jew in the eyes of God. Jesus died for them all! After seeing America through the eyes of a Rabbi, and his wife, it seems that the churches of America need to see a vision to show us that Jesus died for the homeless as well and they must stop being invisible to us. They are special enough for Him to die for them.

CHAPTER 4

NOW IN THE midst of what appears to be a refusal to notice the hurting, there are ministries going on around the country. Some are quite small at this time, but they are quite effective as well. I wish I knew all of them so I could put them in my book so all of you would know of them, because sometimes we get to feeling like the prophet Elijah who thought he was the last of God's people in Israel (1 Kings 19:10). Sometimes when you look at the entire problem, you can fail to see God at work in different areas.

One such ministry sprang up recently in Alton, New Hampshire. I was asked to speak at a small church being pastored by Sam Huggard, a great young pastor with a truly compassionate heart. God, once again, showed me His sense of humor when raising up ministries. Sam invited me to come and share my ministry to the homeless. He said, "I would love to have you come and inspire my church to do something in this area of compassion ministry." Of course, we both knew I couldn't inspire anyone to do anything. I had already "uninspired" most of my congregation to leave the church, because of my bringing the homeless in to live at the church. But I knew what he meant and went to speak and waited to see how his church would respond. I heard from Sam a short while later. I still smile when I recall our conversation. He said, "Richard, a family did get inspired to do compassion ministry. But it was my wife and I!" You've gotta love how "Dad" works. It's kind of like the old candid camera show which proclaimed "Look out, because when you least expect it you will find yourself on candid camera." Sam and his wife were led by Jesus to sell their home and purchase an old nursing home. They decided to fix it up and make an apartment in another part of it. Their goal is to take in a hurting family and work with them to get them back on their feet. Sam shared with me that they are currently up and running and have already taken in their first family. Now Sam's church also got involved in the project. They put together crews to do the repairs and many donated to the project, as well.

Sam does not take in 100 people at a time, but God showed me how He can take care of the hurting in America one family at a time if His people will listen to Him and be inspired to do what they can. Like Elijah, God has shown me I am not alone in this battle to care for the homeless, hungry, and hurting. I simply can't see all the ministries He is using to eventually get the job done.

I received a call from a man in Odessa, Florida, who wanted to tell me he read my book and it encouraged him in his ministry to the homeless. Bob and Brenda of the Messengers of Hope Ministry decided to feed and clothe the homeless in their area. They do not have a building yet, and he was not pastoring a church, so he couldn't do what we did at Trinity. They felt led to take a bag of items to people living on the streets. He shared how they packed up 100 bags to hand out to the homeless. He told me how it felt to get hugged by a homeless person. He said, "It is like getting hugged by Jesus!" He described them as dirty, unwashed, and having some body odor, but he shared with me that this is more than likely how it was to hug Jesus in His day. He was homeless for three years, traveled around by foot in a hot climate, and did not have a shower handy on a daily basis. What a privilege it would have been to hug Him in that condition. Imagine, those "invisible" and sometimes smelly individuals could have been Jesus himself 2000 years ago. We need more people thinking like that.

Now, not everyone responds in the same manner as Sam and Bob. I contact pastors regularly to get permission to come and speak about the miracles of Jesus as we work in this homeless ministry. I will never forget my conversation with one particular pastor. I called him and told him who I was. He replied, "I know who you are and I know all about your ministry to the homeless. I heard you speak at a conference." I was thinking, "Cool. I have a live one on the line here!" But, I have to admit that I was soon shocked and dismayed. Actually, what I heard next truly hurt my heart on the level of when my congregation walked out, not desiring to worship with "those kind of people." This is what he had to say to me. "No, I do not want you to come here to speak and I will tell you why. You speak and people get excited and inspired to work with the homeless. I do NOT want anything to do with the homeless, nor do I want my people involved with them, either." You see, I have come to love "those kind of people" and that hurt my heart to hear it expressed that way. Perhaps others who did not invite me to speak felt the same way, but did not express it to me in such a fashion. But, I have to admit he was honest with me. If my heart hurt, I wonder how Jesus felt when those words were uttered by a man claiming to represent Him! The words of Rabbi Solomon are ringing in my ears as I still hear him proclaiming what he saw in America. And that will only change when we have more compassion for and less judgment of "those kind of people." I wonder if the same people who have no compassion for the hurting are wearing a bracelet with WWJD on it. That stands for What Would Jesus Do, and I can assure you that He wouldn't see them as invisible, and that is shown by the ones being inspired to do something, whatever that may be!

God has raised up another neat little compassion ministry in a small church in rural Maine. It is pastored by an old friend, Pastor Steve Nute, who has a huge heart for the hurting. His church is Nealley's Corner Church which consists of a small congregation with huge giving hearts. They started by heading up a ministry for hungry children in other countries, but quickly added a ministry to local people who were hungry as well. I know they want no credit for what they do, but they did spearhead a drive that brought in $30,000 to buy food for the hungry. One means of accomplishing that was to hand out M&M

candy containers into which you could fit quarters. It is amazing how people putting their quarters together can accomplish so much for the cause of Christ and compassion. Children and folks on social security can contribute in this way and feel great about helping those less fortunate. Once again, Jesus shows us how He can supply great needs when His people are moved to give even a little. All you need is a heart that is softened towards others to be a major part in the mission of compassion that causes others to be "Sheltered by Jesus."

CHAPTER 5

THROUGH THE YEARS God has raised up some incredible people who amaze you when you are privileged to meet them. During this ministry, God has blessed me by allowing me to meet some of those people. They would never have to wear a WWJD bracelet, because when you meet them their lives scream out, "This is exactly what Jesus would do!"

I would like to introduce you to a sweet, little elderly lady named Audrey. This lady has such a heart for the homeless she gave bread from a tiny bakery that hardly made enough to purchase materials with which to bake. She would call regularly every Friday to be sure we would pick up bread at her house. I have been to her house in the winter when it was so chilly inside you needed to go outside to get warm. She turned the thermostats down to the point it kept things from freezing in the house and not much more than that. She did it so she would have some money to help provide for the homeless. I have heard the expression, "I get a warm fuzzy when something in particular happens." That would be the only type of "warm" in her house, and I have never once heard her complain. She was always simply concerned with how I was doing and how the homeless were doing. She even planted a tiny garden and gave to the homeless from it. I've heard her state many times, "I wish I could give more, but if every believer and every church would give a little, we would be able to take care of the homeless." I have to ask myself, how was God able to put a 10-foot heart into a 5-foot body? It is this type of selflessness that can turn the American Church around and make it something "Dad" could be proud to claim as His own.

I got a call from my friend Jeff Hodges and he told me of a man who he believed would like to join me in the homeless ministry. He began by saying, "Don't judge what he can do by the condition in which you will find him." An interesting way to start a conversation. He then told me his name was Ricky Garland and he was suffering from M.S. He said that Ricky was in a wheelchair and uses crutches to some extent. But, he added, that Ricky was quite resourceful and always figured out a way to get things done. So we set up a time to meet. When I met Ricky he was attempting to move around on crutches and it was a major effort to do so. His legs were bent sideways in a very awkward position. His body was not very impressive, but his attitude was off the charts. He shared how he had a burden for the homeless and was ready to go to work in any capacity needed. I watched him mingle with the homeless and saw him become like a magnet to them. It was love at first sight. That inspired me, but I saw and heard other things that impressed me even more. His attitude about Jesus was amazing. He never once complained about his physical problems. I knew God sent him to rub off on those who may whine about their plights. They could tell me that I don't fully grasp the pain of what they are experiencing, but that was not going to fly with Ricky. I remember the first service he attended like it was yesterday. The worship team begin to pray and invited all who were able to stand to do so. I have to chuckle as I remember what happened next. A handful of the residents stood up, but not too many. When they first come to the shelter and find themselves forced to be in the service, they are not always immediately excited. But all of a sudden Ricky grabs hold of the chair in front of him and with tremendous effort pulls his bent body into a standing position. With one hand now firmly placed on the chair, he raised the other to praise Jesus! Let me tell you, my eyes began to leak and I wasn't the Lone Ranger, either. Then all over the room the residents rose to their feet to join him standing to praise the Lord. The next day, we discussed his role in this ministry. He was going to make contacts to encourage support, and he was going to take over the golf tournament we do as a fund-raiser, along with teaching bible studies for the residents. He was a man of great faith and courage with a desire to serve his God. He shared with me how he wanted to find a Christian lady, get married, and have children. He dreamed the same dreams as everyone else. But before any of this came to fruition, he was at his father's camp that was located on a lake, getting it prepared for the summer renters. Somehow, Ricky fell off the wharf while in his wheelchair and died. He is Sheltered by Jesus now. The Lord's gain is our loss. We need more Ricky's to inspire us to think of others more than ourselves, to truly look at the homeless and see them as hurting human beings and not simply the invisible ones for whom we have no time. God brings these special "angels" into our lives to teach us. Of course, he does!

I wish Ricky was here to get the phone call I got last night. A man called to say he has M.S. and is on crutches. He said, "I am sitting in Walmart in Augusta with no money, nobody, and no place to go." He had called a lot of shelters and was unable to get into any for the night. The store would close soon and he would have to move that hurting body out onto the streets for the night. One shelter told him to call every hour on the hour through the day and they would tell him the status of taking him there to stay. The final call was at 6:00pm when he called and heard these words, "Sorry, but we just gave away our last bed." Ricky would've done something, somehow to care for a man in his own condition. He would have found a way somehow, because he would have cared! I'm sorry, but there is NO excuse for leaving a man in his condition without any help or hope! We have been way over capacity many times, but just lay a mattress on the floor and bring them inside. We sent our truck to get him and drove by the ones who said "No." We need more Ricky's and Audrey's, and so many others who put others ahead of themselves. Those who can't sleep nights in their own comfort while others are crying for help without any comfort, even the barest of necessities.

CHAPTER 6

Jesus has blessed me with the privilege of traveling to share some of these marvelous stories. You know what's really nice about it all, is that I do not have to come up with anything. I simply am privileged to share the accounts of what takes place. What's truly amazing is the fact that I can hardly believe some of these things myself. I do not know why Jesus called me to do all of this. I feel like the man who was blind and Jesus placed mud on his eyes and when he washed it off he could see (John 9:13-25). The Pharisees asked him about Jesus doing this. They asked if he believed Jesus to be from God or a sinner. I love his simple answer. "I don't know. One thing I do know, I was blind but now I can see!" I have no more explanation as to why I get to "see" these great things today. They just continue to happen and all I can do is travel and tell the truth of what Jesus is accomplishing.

For instance, James 5:13-20 proclaims if you are sick, ask to be anointed with oil and prayed over and you will be raised up. I do not grasp how all this works. I have anointed and prayed over many in my ministry. They did not all get healed. I do not have the gift of healing, but for some unknown reason Jesus decided to show me His power. In all honesty, it shocked the daylights out of me.

One day, I got a call from Gary in Loudon, New Hampshire. It was an unusual phone call for me. Gary told me that a group had been praying about Jesus doing a healing on their group. He went on to say, "You are speaking at our church in a couple of weeks, and we feel led to ask something of you. When you come, you will be staying at my home and I would ask that you bring some oil and anoint us in our group, and pray over us for healing." If you read my first book, "Sheltered by Jesus: A Voice for the Homeless," you read about a healing of throat cancer suffered by one of our residents. Even after experiencing that, I struggle with how God chooses to heal.

We gathered in Gary's living room and began to pray asking Jesus to please touch someone with healing. What happened next blew me away. All of a sudden, I felt electricity was running through my body. I found myself simply crying out, "Thank you, Jesus. Thank you, Jesus." It was the most amazing feeling ever. I laugh when I recall what happened next. Remember, I don't have the gift of healing and with me standing there all emotional and "doing nothing," my wife hollers at me, "Will you touch someone before you lose it?" I remember placing oil on Gary's forehead and asking Jesus to heal him. Now, Gary has been suffering with pain for over a year, and has been receiving treatments for cancer. As soon as I touched him, he cried out, "The pain all stopped." Being the great man of faith that I've become, I didn't believe it! I believed the emotions of the moment caused such adrenaline to flow that he couldn't feel the pain. The next day, we get up and he hugs me, and with excitement in his voice proclaims, "This is the first day in over a year I am pain free." I replied, "That's really nice, Gary," but I'm still not convinced.

The next day, Monday, he went to his appointment for his cancer checkup, got his blood tests, and x-rays. That evening, he gets a call to come in for more tests, because nothing had shown up in the blood tests or x-rays as it had before. The doctor told him he had no answer for it, but he was cancer free. Gary said, "I told him Jesus healed me and the doctor simply went silent." Gary shared how many refuse to believe he's healed, but time has passed without any pain or signs of cancer. How do I explain what Jesus did that night in Gary's living room? I can't! All I know is the man had cancer and now he is healed, and as Forrest Gump would say, "That's all I got to say about that!" Gary requested to be in my next book, which is this one, because he wanted to be sure Jesus got the glory He deserved for healing him. Well, Gary, here it is my friend. Praise the Lord!

I found myself in another situation where "Dad" wanted to show off His powers to heal. I do believe this instance had two purposes, #1: obviously to heal in answer to prayer, #2: to keep boosting my faith so I will hang in there in what I would call impossible situations.

One day I was speaking at the Windsor Locks Congregational Church in Windsor Locks, Connecticut. I was approached by Pastor Kevin Flannery and he shared a story of a young man who was in the hospital following an accident and given no chance of survival. I was asked by a family member, Scott, to visit and pray for him. This young man, Shawn, was one who had worked on the building of our men's shelter. We called him Monkey, because he would go up and down the building without a ladder. I think I pulled a muscle watching him jump off the roof to the ground. He was in incredible physical condition, so to hear of him in this condition was shocking to say the least. I had come to love this young man, which made it even tougher. When I arrived at the hospital, the family was there and a nurse was with them. Together, they relayed the facts of what had happened, the condition he was in, and what to expect for an outcome. None of it was pretty.

The side of his head was crushed, so it looked like the fender of a car that had just been in an accident. He had tubes everywhere and was basically kept alive by a machine. The prognosis was as grim as it could be, at least from a medical standpoint. I was told by the nurse that he most likely would not survive much longer, and if indeed he did by some miracle, he would be a vegetable in a nursing home. He would never again feed himself, be able to talk or walk. This is not what I wanted to hear about this young man.

I put a hand on him and began to beg Jesus to heal him. I believe He raised Lazarus and he had been in a tomb for four days (John

Chapter 11). Something weird happened while I was praying, not like with Gary when I felt like a human fireworks went off with him. This time, however, I felt something and goosebumps began to pop up all over my body. All of a sudden, I knew he wouldn't die or be a vegetable. Now, if you do not believe this, I understand because it sounds wild, even as I write it down, but it happened just this way.

I turned to speak to Scott, and the nurse was there to hear the conversation. I said, "Scott, he is going to make it." I could hardly believe these words were coming out of my mouth! It sounds crazy, and it felt crazy at the time. I'm crying now, and so is Scott. Ronnie (my nephew I wrote about in my first book) joins in and cries along with us.

The nurse asks if she can speak with me alone. As soon as we are out of ear shot, she lets me have it in no uncertain terms. She said, "How could you do such a thing to this family? We have prepared them for the inevitable, and you just gave them false hope. That's horrible!" Now, I understand her frustration. She is a medical professional who has seen this many times and has seen what normally transpires. If all things were equal, she would have been 100% correct. But, I've seen things she has never seen. I've seen real miracles happen before my eyes. I've stood in her shoes, doubting that a positive outcome was even possible, so I get it. Believe me, I do get it, but Jesus has taught me to look beyond the normal, beyond the possible, and look for Him to show me, and everyone else, that He is God.

Well, to keep a short story long, Jesus had something special on the way. I'm sure you figured that or I wouldn't be putting this story in my book. Down the road from this day, we were having our Grand Opening of the new men's shelter. A couple of the men from the Windsor Locks Church came, as Pastor Kevin Flannery was to be one of the speakers, and they said "We have a surprise for you." Guess who they brought with them in a wheelchair without any life support? You guessed it! Shawn was there, and he "spoke" with me. His speech was slow, but he was speaking. They had done surgery to the side of his head and it looked normal. I had myself another good "Jesus cry!" What Jesus had led me to believe to be possible that day in the hospital had come to fruition and was there before my very eyes. I had not given false hope to the family. Jesus made me look real good that day, and not like a fool!

To top this story off, I went to speak at Windsor Locks at a later date, and guess who was greeting and passing out bulletins at the door. You are a great guesser! Yes, it was Shawn! I do not know how it will all turn out in the end. He may or may not walk, but I do know that at this point he is alive, eating on his own and talking. He beat all the odds, and that's how it works when Jesus decides to go against all human wisdom and once again proves He is God!

When you read this, please don't think, hey, let's call Pastor Berry to pray over all the sick so they will get healed. Two great reasons for that, #1: I do not have the gift of healing. These are isolated cases that

Jesus chose to do for whatever reason, and #2: God has shown in scripture He does NOT heal everyone physically. In 2 Corinthians Chapter 12, Paul explains how he had this "thorn in the flesh," whatever that may have been. He pleaded with God three times to take it away with zero results. God did explain to him, however, that it was for his own good. I am not a great theologian, so I will leave it to the intellectuals to fight over the meaning. But, for a simple ol' country boy preacher, I still grasp the truth that no matter who it is praying, God heals as He chooses and no matter what the results may be, they will always be for our best and His glory.

CHAPTER 7

I HAVE BEEN blessed to see a variety of ministries that may or may not be connected with homelessness, but shows off the heart of God.

I went to speak in Byron, Illinois, to a small group of people with a huge heart. I had become friends with Pastor Gary Cortese, Jr. We communicate over the phone on a regular basis. He has a tremendous heart's desire to do something in the line of compassion ministry. While I was there having supper with Gary, our wives, and some church members, we decided to pray and seek how "Dad" would use this small body of believers to show His love for the hurting. Like Bob and Brenda, his church did not own a church building. They rented a community building for which to hold services. So again, they could not take in the homeless in the same manner as we did at Trinity. I finished praying and Gary proclaimed the Holy Spirit showed him a ministry while I was praying. He began to share how he knew of a couple of young ladies who were pregnant and no one was offering any help. There were no family members, friends, or churches stepping up to help them. We began to brainstorm and expected the Holy Spirit to guide us to how they could receive help in their situation. You know it's easy to judge and condemn, but not so easy to offer aid. The decision was made to begin with offering to do a baby shower for the young ladies. When the discussion started, names were flying of ladies who could help. I was thrilled at their attitude. They were showing the love of Jesus to those who had not seen much of it to this point.

If you are not careful, acts of love can spring up like wildflowers in the springtime. If every tiny church took on a small compassion ministry, we would see a revival in action instead of constantly praying for it. Revival will come when we roll up our sleeves and go to work, loving and caring as Jesus did.

In Beacon Hill Evangelical Free Church in Monroe, Connecticut, I've had the privilege of speaking many times while watching them grow into the idea of helping us. I spoke at a Vacation Bible School there, and the children were awesome. At the closing ceremony, they collected a huge sum of money, which was great, but their testimonies touched me even more. When they realized that homeless children did not have the types of things they took for granted, they were moved to do something on an individual basis. I remember vividly one little girl standing up and asking what the beds were like at the shelter. She was blown away to learn that they were simply 2"x6' boards screwed together with a piece of plywood to hold the mattress, and even more shocked to learn the whole family lived in one room. Then they began to stand up and offer some of their stuff for the children. Some offered clothing, some offered toys, and others inquired about special things the children could use. Wow, could the pastors, leaders, and congregations in America learn a few lessons from the hearts of these little ones! Scripture was being lived out before my very eyes. Acts 2:44-45, "All the believers were together and had everything in common. Selling their possession, and goods, they gave to anyone as he had need." It's so simple for the churches to handle the homeless, hurting, and hungry. Simply follow the way of the first church and these present day believers in small bodies. Just before we left, we were called up front and these children actually laid hands on me and my wife and prayed for us and our ministry. They prayed these little homeless children would have all they needed. I've had hands laid on me in the past, but never by a group of children. I wish I could express how that made both my wife and I feel, but I would fail miserably to convey our emotions. "Dad" is at work, preparing a new generation to take on the challenges neglected by ours.

CHAPTER 8

I JUST GOT a call from a case manager on behalf of a man getting out of jail in a month. He was calling to see if we could reserve a bed for this man. I quickly informed him that we do not reserve beds. The reason being that we never turn anyone away due to a shortage of beds. We simply drop a mattress on the floor until we have a bunk available in a room. The thing that amazes people when they tour our facility is when they see the mattresses. They are up against the walls in the dining room, and if that is full, then we put them in the sanctuary. New folks coming to the church for the first time are quite amazed with the sight of mattresses up against the walls.

As I travel and speak at other churches, I see things I label as "bells and whistles." You walk in and it looks like how you would picture a church to look like today. Nice neat sanctuary, usually with a nice sound system, communion table, etc. Not a thing wrong with it and I am not insinuating that it is wrong. I remarked one time at church when I was preaching at home and noted that we do not have many "bells and whistles" in the sanctuary. I was promptly told in no uncertain terms, "Pastor, we have the very best of "bells and whistles" in this sanctuary!" He began to point to all the mattresses up against the walls and then proclaimed, "I believe these to be the greatest of all the "bells and whistles!" Then Brian, who is in a wheelchair at this time, and who was at one point homeless, made me a board on which he actually hung bells and whistles! That board was presented to me in a service and the place erupted with applause. Brian proudly proclaimed to me, "There, Pastor. You can no longer say you lack "bells and whistles" in your church."

You know Jesus has a sense of humor and it comes out of his people at some weird, but special times. I wouldn't trade any of my 'bells and whistles" for the fanciest sanctuary in the entire world. God bless our "bells and whistles," and he surely does! Of course, he does!

I truly marvel at how people are beginning to come to a church that has homeless people and mattresses on the wall. Believe it or not (I guess I am speaking to myself at this point), Jesus is bringing in replacements for the 80% who left. He's reaching out, by the Holy Spirit, to draw those seeking to serve and not seeking to be served. It seems that, Christians especially, "check out churches" when they move into a new area. I get asked some of the same questions over and over by the "church seekers." How large is your church? What type of music do you play? Where do you stand on the King James Version of the Bible? What is your youth group like? Do you have men's and ladies' bible studies? Do you have a dress code? I'm sure most people may view these as important, and to some extent they are. How many times, though, do you ask, Can I help in some way? Will I be allowed to serve? Are you serving the community? Do you have programs that I can help with to show compassion to the community? Sorry if this sounds too controversial, but I honestly believe that the things which are most important to Jesus need to begin to be more important to us. Jesus Himself said the two greatest commandments are simply to love God with all we are and all we have (my paraphrase), and to love our neighbor as ourselves (Luke 10:27). When things about a church become more important to us as a standard to attend there or not, then something is radically wrong with how we "do church!" Why can't we be known as "others-servers," and not as "self-servers?"

CHAPTER 9

I HAVE BEEN blessed to travel and share the miracles of Jesus that are happening on a regular basis with this homeless shelter ministry. I get to meet some fantastic people who truly love Jesus and desire to see some miracles themselves, but mostly desire to witness some salvations. I know I couldn't wait to go to bible school at Maine Bible Institute, learn how to teach the Word of God properly, and reach people with the gospel so they could get to know and love Jesus as I did. I truly doubt anyone who has felt led to go to bible school and serve Jesus ever felt much different about it. I can hardly speak for myself most of the time, let alone speak for others, but this is how I feel so that's why I'm making this statement.

I see and hear the same basic things most of the time. We want to see people coming to Jesus. But, I had a gentlemen make a statement that summed up pretty much what I see and hear as I travel. He said to me, and to others who were present following a service in which I shared how we saw more than 400 come to believe in Jesus in 2015, "I have been attending this church for 15 years and can't remember one person coming to Christ." Wow, that was a real grabber! I mean, as my grandfather used to love to say, "Hey, boys, that statement could grow hair on a cue ball!" I have never seen hair growing on a cue ball, but if it were possible I believe that statement would start the process. So, what's the problem? Why aren't people simply coming into a church when the doors are open on Sunday so they can hear the words of Jesus spoken and give their lives to Him?

I do not claim to be the "Great Answer Man," but the difference between us and them is that the doors are open all week and there is something else offered to get them to desire to hear the gospel. To get them to ask the question, "Why are you doing this for me?" Then we get to share how Jesus loves them and that's why we love them. It's a simple answer to the questions asked, but you can't answer a question that is never asked. So, I was asked the question I am often asked as I travel and speak... What can our church do in our neighborhood? Being the brilliant individual with a quick wit that I possess, I quickly give this answer... "I don't know!" Every community is different. But, every community is also the same. Not all have a street full of homeless, but all have a community full of hurting people. Ask Jesus for the wisdom to discern the needs and to supply what is needed to meet those needs. I promise you all people are alike in the area of wondering why you care so much. When you tell them the reason is Jesus, I doubt very much that it will take another 15 years before you see a salvation in your church. The formula has not changed in over 2,000 years. In Acts 2:42-47 we read that the early church, "…gave to everyone as they had need…and the Lord added to their numbers daily those who were being saved." Each church needs to find the needs and meet them, and leave the rest up to Jesus. If we begin to do this in America, I believe we will see a revival that will look like the great revivals of the past.

While I was speaking at a church, a man came up to me afterward to share how God had spoken to him while I was preaching. He told me how moved he was to hear the stories of the families, with children, living in our church at this time. He said, "When you shared how you are going to build a family shelter so the children will be able to stay in a safe place with their mom and dad, Jesus spoke to me. He said, 'You have toys that could be sold to bring in support for families who have nothing.'" I just love it when Jesus does that stuff! The next week he drove up to my shelter on a 1997 Harley Davidson "Fat Boy" motorcycle. It only had 34,000 miles and looked like he must have kept it in his own bed to keep anything from touching it. It was a gorgeous bike! His wife followed him to the shelter to give him a ride home afterwards. He shared how he told her the story of the little children and he believed God spoke to him, so she agreed that they should part with the bike as well. He stopped along the way to have it inspected and to change the oil. Then he proceeded to give me the title, told me not to say who donated it, and then he and his wife road away like the Lone Ranger and Tonto!

It never ceases to amaze me how God speaks to those who have a sensitive spirit to hear Him. There are so many stories, and I know I will leave out many that have transpired since we began this ministry. But, another one has just come to mind and I would love to share it with you.

One day Tinker came to my office to share some bad news. He drives our pickup truck for the deliveries from the markets. He said, "I hate to tell you this, Pastor, but the old truck just died." We had no "truck fund" lying around, or any money, at that time. He had a little old truck so he said he would use it until we got something. That created two problems, #1: his truck was on its death bed under hospice care, and #2: only Jesus knew how long it would be until we had enough money to buy another one. My treasurer explained very clearly that we were broke, a common condition we had learned to accept as "normal" over the years. But, Jesus was already speaking to the heart of a man who loved the homeless ministry. I doubt seriously that he would want his name mentioned, either, so I will leave it that a man moved by God showed up in my office. He walked in and quickly stated, "I hear you need a truck." I replied, "Yup, and we need to purchase one without having any money!" He said, "Look out your office window and tell me what you see." I looked and saw his truck that he drove every day, a very nice truck on which he had already purchased four new tires and a sticker. He asked, “Would that do the job for you?” I quickly came back with, “We don’t have enough money to afford that truck.” He tossed me the keys, and with a huge smile proclaimed, “You need to give me a ride home because I no longer have a vehicle.” Isn’t God amazing?

CHAPTER 10

IN THE MIDST of miracles and mayhem, things happen at the shelter that are hard to describe and do them justice. I just thought that in the middle of this book I would like to write about some funny and weird things.

My wife has this thing about cracks showing. Now, I do not mean the ones in the road, so you get my drift. At the shelter, we take in people with problems. Some deal with alcohol, drugs, anger, depression, suicide, handicapped in a wheelchair, missing legs, etc., so sometimes a little laughter goes a long way!

I remember one day in particular when she pointed out a young man and asked me to speak to him about his "crack problem," and I do not mean drug addiction! He seemed to believe it was cool to wear his belt below the equator, or was simply too lazy to pull up his pants. Well, I relayed that message to him a few times to no avail. One day, he was bent over picking up something and my wife had reached her limit of patience. There was a water hose hanging beside the church, and now she was about to be armed and dangerous. Guess what she had in mind? Yup, she ran and grabbed that hose without his knowledge, since his back was turned to her. The next thing I know, she has that nozzle aimed at the "crack target," and then she pulled the trigger. You never saw so much water come down a pant leg, and the pants were coming up as he was running away in the parking lot. I tell you what, the next time he saw that five feet of terror coming his way, he checked to be sure the "crack problem" was not in plain sight. We may have to start a class, taught by my wife, entitled "cracks anonymous," or "the consequences that come from keeping your pants at half-mast!"

Sometimes it is not only the residents who pay a price for bringing laughter to our shelter. I remember another day that caused me to wind up at the wrong end of the laughter. A lady came into my office and proceeded to ask me if we carried "special supplies." Now, you have to understand I do not have women in my office if I am alone, so there was an audience for this one. She came right up to my desk, leaned over and said, "I have a woman problem." Being a truly "dumb hick" at that particular moment, I went ahead and inquired what it was she needed. She said, "Pastor, I need feminine products. Do you happen to have any here?" Now, I never even asked who sent her to my office, because she was new to the shelter, but I have female staff and she chose to ask me! My face gets red even as I write this, and all I can say is Jesus must have a major sense of humor, because He raised up this shelter and stuck me in it. I know I haven't suffered for the gospel as many do all over the world, but this has to rank up there somewhere! If you want to be a pastor at a shelter, the first qualification is a sense of humor.

Sometimes things happen that are truly difficult to paint the picture so that you get the full effect. I guess I should qualify that by stating that when dealing with folks through the shelter, always be prepared for things which you can't be prepared, if that makes sense, and it probably does not!

One day I get a request from this couple who used to be in the shelter. They were boyfriend and girlfriend at that time. I get a call from them declaring to me she is now 8 ½ months pregnant and they want the baby to be born with married parents. They shared how they had no money and wanted to know how much I charge to do a wedding at the church. Since they already stated they have no money, it does not take a rocket scientist to grasp the fact they can't pay for a wedding. Therefore, I agreed to do the wedding at the church for free. I explain we need to meet ahead of time so I can counsel them about marriage. At the time they come, we discuss marriage roles as laid out in scripture. We also discuss what the wedding will be like. I asked if they had music they wanted played, and they stated they did not. There is an area that I would have discussed had I been told ahead of time, and that is what they are going to wear. You might be thinking to yourself the same thing I would have, "What difference does that make?" If that is what you are thinking, I want to make this statement, "How naïve you are as well!"

When they showed up for the wedding, it was an amazing sight. She had bought the bridal gown before she was pregnant. You might be thinking, "So what? Dresses can be altered to fit." Yes, they can, but this one was NOT altered. The back was wide open down to her waist, and she was showing her bra! I have no words to describe it. Now, you would think it would not get worse, but you would be wrong. As she "gracefully" moved down the aisle, two things happened that caught me off guard, and with this shelter ministry you would think I have gotten past that by now. From underneath the gown, her feet appear in green crocks! Plus, those in attendance all of a sudden decided we should play "Here Comes the Bride," and since there was no recorded music, musicians, or singers, they began to hum the tune loudly! I wound up doing a wedding inspired by what sounded like a room full of kazoos! Now, do that and look pastoral in the midst of it all! Note: you will not survive in a homeless shelter ministry without a great sense of humor!

CHAPTER 11

I WOULD LIKE to show off for the homeless for a moment. We continue to deal with the same old question, "How does your wife feel about living next to those people?" I have responded in the past with, "Come onto this property and attempt to bother my wife, and see what you face as consequences. You would do well to make it off the property in one piece!" Now, some property is protected by dogs, but if we put up a sign it wouldn't say "Beware of the dogs," it would say "Beware of her guys!"

I want to go on record as saying it is much more than protection that they offer to her. They love her, and show their appreciation at different times and in different ways. One such demonstration happened on her birthday. A man who had won $2,000 wanted to tithe it to the shelter, so he showed up and handed me $200. He told me it was for the residents to spend on whatever they desired. We only sheltered men at that time, so the discussion involved things the men liked. They asked me for advice, and my advice was "Don't ask my advice." I told them I wanted no part in influencing them, because the donor wanted them to spend it on whatever they chose.

It was really funny to listen to them as they debated how to spend the money. The usual things were discussed, such as pizza, cigarettes, coffee, ice cream, etc. Each time they took a vote, someone would vote against whatever the item was that had been brought up. That lasted an entire day, believe it or not. I came into the shelter in the morning and they approached me with a question and then a statement. They asked if it was true that my wife had never had a birthday party, even as a child. I told them it was true. They went on to explain their failure to decide where to spend the money until one man made a motion to throw my wife her first ever birthday party, and gave her an envelope with the entire $200 in it. They hadn't spent one cent of that money on themselves. You can answer the question for me. How does my wife feel about living next to "her guys?"

CHAPTER 12

I GUESS IT has become quite obvious to you by now that this homeless ministry is made up of all types of people. They arrive in all kinds of different conditions. Some make you laugh, some make you cry, and some just leave you with a feeling that is very hard to describe. I know that over these past few years, God has brought people into my path that send my emotions on a roller coaster. Most of the time, I know what to say, or do, to deal with the situation. But I have to admit, that sometimes words seem to simply fall short, at least in my own estimation.

One situation occurred that left me with a sick feeling in my stomach that still has not fully gone away. I received a phone call from another pastor one afternoon. He informed me that a family stopped by his church seeking help. They were with a group and were abandoned. He shared how it was close to evening service time, so he needed to get them out before the service started. He shared how he had no means to care for them, and asked if I could take them. He said, "You understand that I can't help them!" I said I would make room for them, so he brought them to me and returned in time for his service. You might be asking yourself, "Why did that affect you so? You take in homeless, don't you?" The answer is yes, I do, but this case hurt more than many others, and I will tell you why. One evening while I was sitting out back with my dog, which I did most evenings in the past, they were sitting with me. I do not know why I asked them this particular question, as I usually just ask how they heard about our shelter. But, for some strange reason, I asked a different question. I asked "Why did you go to the church whose pastor brought you here?" I still don't know why I asked that question, but I will never forget the answer. The man said, "We were across the street from that church and we were discussing what to do next. We had no money and were nearly out of food." Then he said, "We looked across the road and saw a large golden cross!" So, he said to his wife and child, "Let's go to the cross. We are sure to find help there!" Wow! I got all choked up and started to cry, but composed myself enough to say, "You betcha, there should always be help when you go to a cross!" Someone stated they loved my first book, because it wasn't "preachy," so I'm sorry if this sounds "preachy," but man alive this is what Rabbi Solomon saw in America. Homeless without help! I do not care what denomination you are, nor do I care about the size of the body of believers, or the size of the building, when someone who is in need comes to the cross, you represent God's love, and you'd better be doing something! It seems we want to go fishing for souls, but when one jumps in the boat we measure it, and if it does not measure up we throw it back! All I can say is if there are more of these families coming to the cross and finding an empty one, Jesus forgive us!

CHAPTER 13

IN THE MIDST of things that break your heart, there rise up things that can make your heart sing. One day while I was in the gym (I know, you couldn't guess by looking at me), a friend inquired if I had any more books to sell. It was for a very special lady with a horrible disease. He works for a social service organization that provides in-home care. He shared how his wife, who is a doctor, was with this lady and asked if there was anything she could do for her. She said, "I've heard of a book called "Sheltered by Jesus" that was written by Pastor Berry, and I would love to have the book. Do you think you could find a copy?" The doctor said, "As it just so happens, the author of the book works out with my husband, so I will have him get you a copy."

Now, by the grace of God, we have sold many books, so that's not what's so special and heartwarming. This lady can't read for herself and this weird disease (I do not know the name of it) does not allow her to even listen for long periods of time. So you know what Jesus did so she could "read" the book? He moved the heart of a lady in our church to go regularly for short periods of time and read it to her. At first, I was not told her name, but I found out through the lady at the church, that lo and behold, she had been in my high school class and we graduated together. My wife and I visited her and she was so excited to share how this book encouraged and strengthened her faith even more than it was already. Isn't it awesome how Jesus gives us these tidbits of encouragement in the midst of the things that break our hearts? Of course, He does, and that is all a part of being "Sheltered by Jesus."

CHAPTER 14

I GUESS I have a tough time grasping how this ministry and my first book, "Sheltered by Jesus, a Voice for the Homeless" affect people. I was speaking at a church and at the end I met a couple that just floored me with what they had to share. They were both elderly and walking, barely, with a cane. While they were waiting for their ride, they said, "We have to share something with you. We read your book and when we heard you were going to speak here today we just had to come and meet you in person." I know the first thing you are thinking is, "What's the big deal about that?" I wouldn't walk across the street to hear me! But what touched my heart about this is they said, "Our health is so bad we have not left our home since last Halloween," and this is now July. If that wouldn't move you, you would have to be made of stone! I have to admit this left me momentarily speechless, and if you knew me you would quickly grasp that to be a miracle all by itself. There is a hunger in the hearts of God's people to hear about miracles today, and this couple was so moved they pushed themselves physically to hear more.

That same day I was approached by two more people who had stories to share with me. One young man was passing out bulletins. His name is Aaron. He had tattoos all over both arms and was wearing short sleeves so they were clearly visible. He asked if I remembered him and I felt terrible because I had to admit that I did not. He told me how he helped with the remodeling of a widow's home, and that widow happened to be my wife's mom. That house should have been condemned, but that's another story. He shared how he was now totally clean, had a job, a home, drove a nice car, and was attending church. He said, "Thanks, because I never would have made it without finding Jesus at the shelter, and having Him clean up my life."

As soon as Aaron stepped aside, a lady came to share her story. She told me she was Will's mom. He was a young man who stayed at the shelter and was truly messed up through addictions. The staff shared how they dealt with him after he swallowed some batteries. Now, that's messed up! But she told me how he has been clean for seven months and has been going to church every Sunday. She asked to hug me before I spoke and then again after I spoke. She just was so overwhelmed with gratitude because she got her son back. "Dad" sure has some awesome success stories!

CHAPTER 15

I WAS PREACHING on John Chapter 11 the other day and I was moved by the question Jesus asked Martha about her brother Lazarus. "Do you believe I can raise him from the dead?" Martha proclaimed she believed he'd be raised up in the last day. But that was not the question Jesus was asking. He wanted to know if she believed He could do it "today." That's the crux of where I see many people in churches as I travel to speak. Almost everyone believes Jesus "can do anything He desires." But, the question of "Can He do it in your life and in your church today?" That seems to be where it breaks down. But every once in a while, Jesus moves someone to believe it can happen today.

There is this couple who has been buying many of my books and passing them out all over the place. I showed up at their home with some books, and Christine asked if she could share a story with me for a change. I was ready to listen intently. I think you will like this one a whole lot.

A lady just got word that she had cancer for the third time. She shared how both she and her husband believed in Jesus, so she did not fear the possibility of dying. But she wanted one thing before Jesus took her home, if He was going to do that. She had grown children in another state that she wanted to see. She faced a problem, however, as she did not have the money for plane fare to bring her children to her home. Her children did not have the funds, either. But she had read my book and saw how I had raised my hands and cried out to my Daddy God and received the miracles. She told Christine, "If He responded to Pastor Berry, then why wouldn't He do the same for me?" So, she shared how she raised her hands and cried out, "Daddy God, please get me the tickets so I can see my children one last time." Before the week had passed, her husband came home from work one day and declared, "You'll never believe what happened to me at work this week! My boss who has never given his employees a bonus decided to do so this week, and I got one thousand dollars." That was what it took to cover the cost of all the tickets! She proclaimed, "Of course, He did!"

CHAPTER 16

I AM SURE you have caught on by now that as I travel and speak, I keep getting amazed at some of the responses. That was never as evident as the one that happened to me recently.

I was speaking at a church in Connecticut and was blessed to see how the folks responded, which is becoming the norm to my utter amazement! As I was closing out my message, a lady cried out from the crowd, "Keep going. We want to hear more of those miraculous stories!" It amazed me as this is a congregation that, when I asked how many of them had heard of me or read my book, NO hands went up! But there was that craving, that desire, to hear more about what Jesus is doing today!

The pastor spoke to me afterwards and confirmed what I had thought about the reason for the crying out for more. He said, "Richard, I want to thank you for bringing the Glory of God to our church!" I was blown away as I am simply a "dumb hick from Skowhegan," and not able to take any glory anywhere. But he said, "Let me explain what I mean by that statement. I am well educated in the Word of God, and so is my church family. They know the Word extremely well, but you did something today, you made the Word real in our time! That's what we need in all our churches." Now that made sense as I know exactly who and what I am. They did not see me as special, but the true stories I shared about "Dad."

It's like the lady who raised her hands to heaven seeking and finding a miracle! Jesus became so much more to her, because she was not simply reading about what Jesus had done for Israel and the early church. She experienced what He will do today when miracles are needed and He is asked to glorify Himself.

CHAPTER 17

HAVE YOU EVER felt like going to the top of a high place and screaming out, "What's wrong with this picture?" Ever have something happen that astounds you to the point of disbelief? Well, I saw a couple of those types of things happen this week.

First of all, a young man named Paul came to the shelter. He shared how he was raised as a Seventh Day Adventist, but when he was old enough, he got some tattoos. He told me how he was looked down upon to the point of leaving what he had grown up knowing. He then tried several other churches in fundamental denominations. He said that he was treated the same way in all of them. Finally, total disheartened, he decided to stay away from churches of any kind. Heard this one before? He then shared how he had been accepted as he was when he came to the shelter. He told me that he appreciated the message of how God seeks relationships more than religion. He realized not only did Jesus accept him, but for the first time since getting a tattoo, the church did as well. This young man is happy to be back in church after years spent away. Jesus is drawing the homeless people together and giving them self-worth, and we need to go out of our way to do the same.

The second thing had to do with a phone call I received this week. It was a social worker in the southern part of Maine. She told me she had a real problem finding a home for this "special little family." It was a young, single mom trying to care for two small children. Now that all by itself is not mind blowing, because unfortunately it is happening all over the country. But what makes her story slightly different is her youngest child, a little girl, is autistic. She is a handful and requires her mom's constant attention. The social worker told me they had been refused by every place she had contacted. Either shelters were full or they did not want to deal with an autistic child at their facility. She said, "Pastor Berry, they are headed for the streets if we can't place them somewhere now. Do you have room, and are you willing to take them in knowing their situation?" I said, "We are full in the family shelter, better known as my church, but I will have my staff scramble things around to take them in today." This should NEVER happen! Both of these cases make me want to scream from the highest place, "What's wrong with us as a country, and churches, when this can happen and we ignore it?" Sorry, but I guess I just got a little bit preachy! My heart breaks for these people and I know the heart of Jesus aches as well! But, we the churches, who carry the name of Jesus can change all of this if we so choose!

CHAPTER 18

I WAS HANDED a story written by Susannah Warner, a lady in my church. She and her husband, Kevin, coach the softball team sponsored by the homeless shelter. In the midst of so many stories of people being ignored or looked down upon, comes this heartwarming story shared by a couple that loves the homeless and the hurting. Her mom actually brought the story to me and asked if I would consider putting it in this book. I guess it is rather obvious what I gave for an answer, as you are about to get to read it.

Trinity has a softball team. Although a church softball team is not unusual for many churches, for a homeless shelter this may seem a bit ridiculous. Most of the players we have had on our team do not have a job, or a home, or even a bed to call their own, so why would God think it is a good idea to encourage them to run around a softball field, chasing balls and swinging bats? Because He loves us and wants us to have fun. Because He knows that not every person who is lost will find their way into a church. Because He seeks us out and comes to where we are. Because He knows how many hairs there are on our heads and so He uses things that we love to draw us to Him. Never has this been more evident than with our softball team this year.

In previous years, we have had plenty of players. Usually, 15-20 young men and women show up to our first practices, some with sneakers and athletic skills, many with cigarettes, most with the energy and the bravado of youth, but none with a bat, ball or glove. The team is unique in that the players come and go throughout the season as some find jobs or get their vouchers for housing and others come in. Some who might have been a home run hitter and star left fielder one week might be gone and could be replaced by a man who has never played the game, but who wants to be a part of the team, or maybe just wants to get out of the shelter for a bit. Because our team is so fluid, we have not had a winning track record by any means. Trinity has always been known throughout the church league as a "Bad News Bears" sort of team. The kind of team that cheers, not when we have won a game, but when we have not lost too badly! For this reason, and because we are disadvantaged in many ways, the league commissioner and other teams have been very kind to us. One team allows us to use their field as our "home field," and games are almost always scheduled there for us instead of on the road, because they realize that transportation can be a problem for us as hardly anyone has a car. Sometimes, if we do have a road game, it requires a ton of work attempting to coordinate rides from nonresidents who attend the games, many of whom are spectators. We have also been given bats and catcher's equipment, and one time a player from the other team brought over two pairs of cleats! They were for the man on our team who was stuck wearing work boots at the time, because he wanted to play and that was all he had to wear. What a huge blessing. You can see that the simple things that you and I take for granted are not so simple for everyone!

This year was a little different. For some reason this spring, there seemed to be far fewer young men and women at the shelter who desired, or were physically able, to play. Having fewer people at a homeless shelter is not a bad thing as a rule, but it causes some difficulties when it comes to fielding a team. Determined to have a team, my husband and I searched outside of the church to recruit some people from town to play. He knew of a group of young men who enjoyed playing softball so much that they organized a pickup game every Sunday. However, these games did not always end well as participants were quite often "three sheets to the wind," and disagreements and fights often ended the play abruptly. Several of these guys were excited about the prospect, even though they were warned that this is a Christian league that would not tolerate drinking, swearing, or smoking on the field, and that weekly church attendance was a league rule. We didn't worry about them following any of the rules, except the last one! At least one of the guys was overheard saying, "Church would probably catch on fire if I went in!" We shouldn't have worried, though, because God provided the answer for us. "Of course, He did!"

One of the guys who was recruited was a huge redhead named Scotty, who is 6'4" and 280 pounds with size 18 feet. He plays left field and hits home runs. Despite his hulking appearance, he is an encouragement to all and is never hard on anyone when they miss the ball, except himself. He is having a rough game one night, early on in our season. He missed a ball he thought he should have been able to catch and was upset with himself. Because of his competitive nature, when the next ball was hit to left field, he ran and dove over a fence in an attempt to catch the ball. The fence tripped him up and this big guy, with all his weight, landed on his side. We all ran over when he did not get right up. We found him struggling to breathe and in obvious pain. He was helped off the field and the decision was made to bring him to the hospital to be checked out. My husband ran to get our Jeep to bring to the field as it was a long walk to the parking lot. While we waited, I asked if we could pray for him. "Yes, please, anything," he said as we gathered around and laid hands on him. We finished as my husband arrived with the Jeep and then went to the hospital. We continued with our game, although we missed Scotty and wondered how he was doing. Later that night we heard that he had been discharged and that nothing was broken. We were relieved to hear this, but a few days later we heard from his point of view what had happened. He said that he was sitting on the stretcher in the ER in pain and struggling to breathe with what he was positive was a broken rib, when suddenly he felt the presence of God. Immediately, the pain was gone and he could breathe normally. He knew that God had healed him and from then on started carrying a pocket bible.

As happy as we were about Scotty, we were concerned about the fact that many of the players were not going to church. We were saddled with the task of telling these excited guys and gals that they either attend church or they couldn't play. Although we knew we needed to be respectful of the league rules, this seemed like a lose/lose scenario. We needed the men in order to play, and more importantly, they were being exposed to the love and mercy of God, all while having a lot of fun. My friend, our scorekeeper, and I were discussing this quandary when she said, "too bad we couldn't bring church to them, you know like a Bible Study." What a perfect, God given idea! Excited by this, she contacted Ronnie who graciously agreed to help us. We told the guys that we would be having a Bible Study before our next game and if they wanted to play, they had to attend. No one balked or complained. In fact, this information was greeted with quiet acceptance.

Before our next game, the whole team sat in the shade, lined up against the back of the dugout like good little soldiers, with Ronnie in a lawn chair facing us. We shared Bibles that I borrowed from the church and helped each other find the scriptures. We took turns reading, even one man who said, "I'll try, but I'm not good at it." All 12 of us, including 2 from the shelter, listened quietly as the Lord, through Ronnie, brought Saul to life with the message that no matter what you have done, you are never too far gone for God. Throughout those 10-15 minutes, everyone was quiet, focused, and listening intently, taking in all the information. After the final prayer, everyone jumped up, ready to play our game, but most shook hands with Ronnie and thanked him. Scott, though, seemed to be the most excited and was heard several times that night saying, "I can't believe this! My mind is blown!" To top off the night, we actually won the game and took celebratory pictures after. Luke 19:10 "For the Son of Man came to seek and save those who are lost."

Since that time, we have continued with Bible studies before games. The players accept this and no one complains, from the 19-year old fresh out of high school to the 55-year old grandfather. Because Jesus has come to where the men are, they have been touched and because we have been given the freedom to observe the spirit of the law, rather than the letter of the law, all have been changed. Scott still carries his pocket bible around and has been known to spontaneously start reading aloud, especially from Psalms. He is the first to remind us that we need to pray after practice, even leading the prayer once, after he said, "I've never done that before and I was nervous!" And our team? We have won more games this year than in all the years as a team combined. "Of course we have!"

Okay, Sue, your story is in the book, and I am so very proud of all of you who lead and play on this team!

CHAPTER 19

I JUST RETURNED from speaking at a gathering in Dresden, Maine. Since I speak at many places, you may be thinking, "So what?" But some special things happened at this gathering. A lady named Barbara (better known to all as "Mother"), got up front and proceeded to state that, "Pastor Joe will be announcing one special guest speaker." Again, nothing special about that. But, it got special in a hurry. He began by saying, "One day my daughter brought home a stray." That "stray" was named Aaron. Pastor Joe went on to share how his daughter fell in love with Aaron. Then he told how Aaron shared with him that he spent time at the Trinity Homeless Shelter in Skowhegan, Maine. It turns out that Aaron is the same Aaron I wrote about earlier in this book! It's not part of that first story, because I just heard this story today. He shared how proud he was of his son-in-law, and how well he and his daughter were doing. I have to admit to getting a little choked up as he dropped this on me just prior to speaking. You talk about Jesus setting the stage for me ahead of time. This gathering was ready to hear much more as soon as Pastor Joe told his story! It's hard to explain how I feel each time I hear of a victory in the life of one of "those kind of people," as many call them. The glory of God was seen and heard on this particular day.

Another strange occurrence happened at that same gathering. What I am about to share you can "believe it or not," as Ripley used to say. I was asked by a lady if she could share something with me after I finished speaking. There was a young man who was autistic and unable to verbally communicate, but he writes and types, so he can communicate very well. He had written on a piece of paper and handed it to the lady who took him in at a young age. She wanted me to read what it said. He had written the following: "I see someone dressed in white and wearing a white veil, standing behind that man who is speaking. Could that be my dead mom?" I can't explain it, but I know how it made me feel. I believe an angel was there as I was speaking and Jesus allowed this special young man the privilege of seeing it. Again, I do not know if you will believe it or not, but when I travel and share about the power and glory of God, crazy things seem to happen for which I have no explanation. Being a "dumb hick," I simply accept these things, and I continue to ask Jesus to not let me get too smart to believe!

CHAPTER 20

GROWING UP, I never gave too much thought of how important it was to actually be able to have a job. Where I grew up there were factories on every corner, and the only ones I knew to be without work were those not desiring to work, and I did not know many of them.

Today, in our area, just desiring a job does not mean there is one for you even under the best of conditions. You may have been to college or trade school, but if a job does not exist that really does not matter.

If you add the small amount of opportunities with drug or alcohol addiction, or a criminal record, the odds of employment come close to hitting rock bottom! That's what many face who wind up at our homeless shelter. We do have those with the education, no records, and yet no jobs. They, of course, are in the minority, but they do exist. That's why every morning at praise and prayer time there is a roar of applause when we hear a resident proclaim with pride, "I just got a job."

It may not be a job that you would scream out, "Praise the Lord!" over, but you would if you wore their shoes for a while.

The other day a young man named Steve walked into my office with a smile the size of the Grand Canyon on his face. He is one who has truly struggled with getting his life on track. He's battled addictions for some time, even though he is still a young man. I have had to discipline him for his failures to abide by the rules many times. I have put him out of the shelter and brought him back many times. You might be thinking, "Why didn't you just give up on him and move on to someone else who would obey the rules?" That's exactly what everyone has done with him for most of his life! But when he entered my office this time (not to be disciplined, by the way), he proudly declared, "Pastor Berry, I got a job! I am stocking shelves at Walmart at night!" It is not a high paying job, and it is not a full time job, but for Steve it is like he won the Megabucks! You need to understand it is not even about the money. It is about the pride of having a job like "normal people." To be able to say, "I'm off to work today!"

You see, I used to take that for granted growing up, but today is a new day, and for these ones it is not to be taken for granted at all. I burst with pride each time a testimony goes up, thanking Jesus for giving something others may take for granted.

CHAPTER 21

If you read my first book, "Sheltered by Jesus, A Voice for the Homeless," you know I shared how my goal for the future was to start a business to put the homeless to work. That is still being worked on with some people looking for ways for us to have a business of our own. But, God has shown me that He is moving hearts to consider employing the homeless.

I was contacted by a group of Christian businessmen called the "Protein Foundation." This group has shown us some support in the past financially. But this time, they approached me with an idea of how to put some of the homeless to work. They oversee an ice cream plant in Michigan called the House of Flavors which has many employees. They have offered to relocate some of our people who may be qualified for one of their many jobs. I got very excited over the prospect of not only a new job, but a new area for some to restart their lives. We are still attempting to bring this to fruition, but we have run into some logistical problems. Our residents do not stay long if they have a desire to get their lives back together, so they find anything they can to get by right now. Some get vouchers for housing and move out before we can finish the employment process with the company. But at least this one opportunity does exist, and I pray one day we will see the first homeless residents start over in Michigan.

What's exciting to me is I see God moving towards opening doors for these people. At least it is a ray of light starting to break through. I know every one of these dear souls is precious to Him, because He died for them. Maybe before I finish this book there will be a breakthrough locally to put them to work. I know it can happen. "Of course it can!"

CHAPTER 22

THERE IS AN old saying, 'Keep the main thing the main thing." Sometimes we drift away from that with our ministries. We attempt to come up with our plans and strategies to move forward and do great things. Then Jesus shows you how simple ministry is supposed to be all along.

Shawn came into my office to shake my hand and say thanks for having this shelter here for him when he was at the end of his rope.

Shawn came to the shelter about two years ago. He was addicted to drugs and alcohol. He was in a hopeless state, to say the least, at the time. But something amazing happened, he found Jesus. The Holy Spirit went to work in his life and over time a tremendous change began to take place. He connected with a mature Christian, Jay, and his family. He began going out to Jay's farm and developed a work ethic, all the while having a godly example to watch. Paul stated in 1 Corinthians 11:1, "Follow me as I follow Christ." Shawn began to do that, and I saw a butterfly come out of a cocoon, spiritually speaking. Jesus had come into this man's life, teamed him up with Jay, took away the desires of his addictions and literally made him a new creature in Christ.

He stood up in church to share his testimony and told how he was clean and sober, that he was moving into his apartment and starting college this fall. He shared how he wanted to study to become a social worker, so he could one day help others like himself.

Credit will be given to many who had a part in his life. The simple truth, however, is all we did was offer him Jesus and let Jesus do His thing. All the fancy ideas in the world, all the conferences and seminars in the world. Boil it all down, and it comes out the same. The method of success in dealing with lives is to show Jesus to them. Share Jesus with them and then let Jesus simply do His thing! To see real transformation is not rocket science. Even a dumb hick from Skowhegan, Maine, can understand it!

CHAPTER 23

SOMETIMES SOMETHING WILL happen that makes me want to scratch my head and ask myself, "Is this really happening?" Today was definitely that kind of moment. You know how there is this movement to get God out of schools, courts, etc.? Well, you may want to ponder what happens next for a few moments.

I had a young man come to me and share something truly amazing. He said, "You know how I have been asking for prayer for my upcoming court appearance?" He had been sharing how he could be facing some serious prison time. So, each morning at prayer time, we asked Dad to steer the judge to show mercy. This young man had been doing so well we put him on our staff. He was impressing us with his work ethic and behavior. But, his past was obviously not as good as what we were seeing every day.

So he heads off to court to find out what his future would hold at the hands of a judge who hasn't seen the changes we've seen. The young man has seen and heard of miracles while at the shelter and is praying for one for himself.

Today he comes to me all smiles and excited. He gets to serve 10 days in the local county jail. Now, for most of us that would be considered anything but exciting! But, he shared what the judge told him. He was sentenced to 6 years in prison. But, instead, he was given 10 days in jail and 1 year with the shelter! Can you imagine that? Wow, the judge sentenced a man to 1 year in church instead of 6 years in prison! The judge told him if he stayed and continued to work at the shelter for 1 year, he wouldn't be going to prison. It's a year of probation so he has to toe the line or do his time!

But, in a nation that is trying to get God out of everything, a judge sees the benefit of how lives are changing through this ministry and sentenced a man to serve a year in the very institution that represents what they are attempting to separate from.

CHAPTER 24

DEALING WITH THE homeless ministry has you reaching the highest of highs and lowest of lows. I have written about so many of the highs, and believe me, they far outweigh the lows. But, you can experience both in the same week.

On the heels of a young man getting "sentenced" to a year in the homeless shelter, we had an incident that sent my emotions the other way. The incident was not all that unusual. A fight happened between a young man and one of my staff. Does not happen often, but the potential is always there for it. People come in a highly emotional state of mind, scared, depressed, suicidal, angry, frustrated, etc. Not difficult to understand when you look at their situation in life.

But the problem is how everything done by someone who is homeless is viewed by those outside the shelter. They are seen in such a manner that anything they do wrong makes the newspaper and headlines, while someone with a home may do the same and it literally goes unnoticed.

This altercation between a resident and staff member made the headlines in our local paper. A writer for the paper called us and asked if I would like to comment on the fact that a homeless person committed a crime. I said "Yes!" My comment was that it made the paper because the person was at the shelter. Altercations go on all over the town and you never read about them. I shared how I was frustrated with how the homeless are treated so differently, and the only difference between them and the others doing the same thing is they are homeless.

Will the way homeless are viewed ever change? The answer is probably never in the eyes of the world. But, it needs to begin to change in the eyes of the church! We need to remind ourselves that Jesus did not die solely for those who had homes!

CHAPTER 25

JUST GOT A call this evening from someone in Waterville, Maine. He asked if we had room to take in a lady he just found on the side of the road. He had been trying to find a place to send her, but all attempts had come up short. He shared how she had been on the street for about three days with no hope of finding a place to go. He said, "She is 70 years old, and has a wheelchair to get around." I do not know any more of the details yet, but I immediately said, 'Yes, we will take her." This is the type of situation that moves my emotions in a great way. One, I praise "Dad" that He has opened up our church to take in those unwanted anywhere else, and two, it hurts my heart that they are NOT wanted anywhere else. Sometimes I wonder if we, as a church, stopped preaching about the Good Samaritan, especially in cases like this one when so many walk past on the other side of the street.

CHAPTER 26

JESUS HAS GIVEN me the privilege of sharing these stories all over the country. What I find amazing is that the Holy Spirit touches hearts and encourages people on every level of life. He touches the "haves," as well as the "have nots."

Just recently I got invited to speak to a group at the Rockefeller Center. As I walked around the city, my mouth and eyes were both wide open. Being a dumb hick from Skowhegan, Maine, the sight of any building over four floors was like Dorothy in the Wizard of Oz! I walked past the "Today Show" being aired as I go to the restaurant to speak to a group of men. My first thought was, "Dad, where are you sending me?" I felt like Moses prior to going to speak to Pharaoh of Egypt. Moses was concerned with his ability to speak and overwhelmed with being put into such a position. I used to wonder how Moses could doubt what God could do with him. I mean, he heard Him speak from the burning bush! What more evidence did he need?

But, I found myself in the same position and questioned God as to whether or not He picked the wrong man for the job. As my "Dad" had done so many times in the past, He did it again. He brought a phrase to my mind that I had never thought of the in the past. A phrase that put all of this into perspective for me was, "My Dad" is the God of the Outhouse and He is the God of the Penthouse! As crazy as it sounds, that caused me to settle down and simply share the miracles Jesus had done at the homeless shelter. God allowed me the privilege to see how He could affect the rich in the same manner as He affected the poor.

It does not matter how the messenger can dress or whether he speaks in fluent "hick." It only matters that the rich and poor alike need to know Jesus loves and forgives them, and is doing miracles in their midst today!

As I travel and share how Jesus loves "those kind of people" as they have been labeled by many. I see my "Dad" bring hope to those hurting over "those kind of people!"

After I spoke at a church in Connecticut, a lady came up to me and shared how her son was going to be homeless due to a terrible drug problem. She loved her son, no matter what he's done or is doing, and asked for prayer and advice. She continues to send me emails concerning her son's progress. She keeps sharing how she has hope, because of her "Daddy" God. Her son would be seen by many as belonging to the "Outhouse!"

I was getting prepared to speak at a church in New Hampshire when a lady approached me. She said, "I do not attend this church, because I live out of the area, but I heard you were speaking so I came because my son just became homeless and I need to find some encouraging words to hold onto at this time! I thought, "Wow. Thanks, "Dad" for allowing me to share how much you love and can miraculously take care of those who seem to have no hope." Somehow the message that Jesus is the "Great I Am" and not the "Great I Was" needs to resound from our churches, and be the reason for hope for all people whether their lives mirror more of the "outhouse" than the "penthouse!"

CHAPTER 27

I HAD THE privilege of speaking at the North Monmouth Community Church in North Monmouth, Maine. Pastor Ed Spencer has done a fantastic job teaching on compassion for the hurting. They have a food pantry that they also shared with our shelter. I truly appreciate the involvement of so many churches. One other thing happened when I spoke at the church, sharing some of the trials, victories, and miracles. I was approached at the end by Seth Roberts. He introduced himself as a filmmaker. He stated that he was going to purchase my book, "Sheltered by Jesus, A Voice For the Homeless," and if it was like my speech he was interested in the rights to make it into a movie. A couple of days later, Seth came to my home with a contract to make the movie. He shared how his whole crew had decided to share any profits from the movie at a rate of 50/50 since all proceeds from the movie go to the homeless shelter, the same as both the books I have written. The movie will be entitled, "Sheltered by Jesus," and by God's grace, be ready to film in 2017. "Dad" never ceases to amaze me how

He works with this shelter to get the message out to encourage others to be a part of a compassion ministry of some sort by others.

Seth called and asked to spend five days getting to meet people in the book and to see the things God had built in so many miraculous ways. While he was at the shelter he also brought along his wife and young daughter Morgana. I watched as that little girl made friends with the homeless children. I remember she made one special friend and the two girls were like they were attached at the hip. You saw one, you saw the other.

Seth shared a story with me when they left. He told how his daughter came to share something with him. She told the other girl she was going to her daddy's car to get something before they left. The little girl looked at her in amazement and said, "You have a car?" Morgana then replied, "Everyone has a car!" The other girl then said, "We don't have a car." This bothered Morgana, so she went to Seth to share this story. Seth said to his daughter, "We need to talk. That little girl does not have a home."

Morgana then said, "Daddy, I've got to do something about that." A couple of weeks later as I sat with Seth approving the script for the movie, he said that his daughter wanted to see me before I left. Morgana came up to me with a "baggie full pennies" she had collected. She proudly proclaimed there were 400 pennies, and she wanted me to give them to that little girl so she could have a home!

I thought to myself, there is hope for the future if the next generation gets moved by "Dad" to do what this little girl did. They won't see them as "those kind of people!"

CHAPTER 28

AT THIS TIME I continue to travel and share the stories, and wait on "Dad" to write the new chapters in the future. We are preparing to break ground in the spring for a new 48-bed family shelter with a playground for children like Morgana's new little friend. We are examining some business possibilities to put the homeless to work while they seek to turn their lives around for the future. We are planning on building a place where we can have our medical clinic and social service offices. We are ready to move forward as "Dad" moves hearts to supply all we need.

One thing He continues to supply are salvations at an incredible rate of more than 400 per year. Perhaps as you read this, "Dad" is speaking to you about how you can be the next Good Samaritan and take part in a compassion ministry in your area, or even join us in ours!

I personally am waiting to see where He will send me with the message of His miracles across America, so more can behold the Glory of God at work in the “outhouses” and “penthouses.” So, I guess all I have left to say is, “the story still continues…”

ABOUT TRINITY HOMELESS SHELTER

Trinity Homeless Shelter is completely staffed by the homeless. WHAT? You read correctly! Many of the folks who have walked in through the doors of this shelter with nothing, are actually running the place! Many have lost jobs and homes, but have found a new lease on life by entering into the shelter, finding purpose and wholeness and giving themselves to the mission and vision of the organization.

This shelter, located in Skowhegan, Maine, could be a template for other churches to follow. The somewhat unorthodox method of having the residents run the facility, feeding, clothing and helping others find gainful employment is nothing short of miraculous...and it works! The staff (residents) gets room and board for their positions. They work in the office, the food pantry, the laundry, kitchen, firing up the wood boiler, and various other chores—all requirements for an on-going operation, so that when the next needy soul shows up at the door, there is shelter from the storm.

If you are interested in learning more, or if you would like to contribute to this unique ministry that has served so many, please visit *shelterbyjesus.org* or write to us at the address below:

Trinity Homeless Shelter
12 McClellan St Ste 2
Skowhegan, Maine 04976

Thank you for your interest in the shelter. I pray that you have been inspired to consider serving wherever God has placed you.

— *Pastor Richard Berry*

ABOUT THE AUTHOR

The Rev. Richard Berry is the Senior Pastor of Trinity Evangelical Free Church and the Skowhegan Miracle Homeless Shelter in Skowhegan, ME. Richard has over 30 years in ministry and holds ordinations with the EFCA and the ABC.

In 2007, Richard was approached by a longtime acquaintance who would be homeless in just a few short days. Richard provided a couch in a church Sunday school room, and the influx of those in need of shelter began crossing the threshold of TEFC. Through the process of housing the homeless in the church, Richard saw 80% of his congregation leave, including immediate family members because they couldn't worship "with those kinds of people." Facing closure from state officials, a dwindling congregation and dwindling finances, Richard simply dropped to his knees and prayed.

Today, through faith and the power of the Living God, a multitude of men, women and children have been provided shelter, food, and spiritual nourishment in the small rural landscape of central Maine through the ministry of Richard and TEFC. The operation is run solely on in-kind donations and the hand of God. The shelter, with a volunteer staff of homeless men, continues to provide shelter to all in need.

The new shelter, with a grand opening in January 2012, boasts a commercial kitchen, commercial laundromat, and a handicap room with oxygen hookup. In addition, the men housed in the ministry have direct access to a free medical clinic each Friday, social and behavioral health services, addiction counseling services, employment services, and an opportunity to gain a seminary level education through the EFCA's Gateway Theological Institute.

The Rev. Richard Berry and the ministry at TEFC has been detailed in several publications including: *Downeast Magazine*, *The Christian Science Monitor*, *The EFCA Today*, several local newspapers and media outlets, as well as local news segments. Furthermore, Richard has been listed in "Who's Who in America" and was honored with the 2010 Crisis and Counseling Agency of the Year award by the State of Maine.

Pastor Berry is available for speaking at your church or group.

Contact him at: *trinity_efree@yahoo.com*

SPONSOR A HOMELESS PERSON

Do you want to be a part of this ministry? This is one simple way ANYONE can help win souls for Christ through this ministry in Skowhegan, Maine. For the price of a few cups of coffee, you can help bring another soul to the Kingdom through what God is doing at this shelter!

Sponsorship:

$108 will provide for one of God's own homeless for an ENTIRE "MONTH" at the shelter:

- Home cooked meals,
- A warm bed,
- Exposure to and instruction in God's Word

For $9/month, your one year contributions can help an individual come off of the street, stand tall, free from HOMELESSNESS with a chance for healing and more importantly a chance to know our God!

☐ 1 Homeless Individual = $9/month or $108/year

☐ 3 Homeless Individuals = $27/month or $324/year

- ☐ 6 Homeless Individuals = $54/month or $648/year
- ☐ 12 Homeless Individuals = $108/month or $1296/year

With your help, we could help take care of those in need that show up at our door throughout the year.

How it works:

1. Choose how many individuals' one month provisions you would like to sponsor.
2. Choose how you would like to give your contributions; monthly or annually.
3. Go to the sponsorship page on our website:

   www.sheltersbyjesus.com

   and there will be a link to donate directly from there.

Feel free to contact us through the website or call the Shelter if you have any questions on this process.

Please contact us for more information if you are interested in sponsoring one or more people. We can automatically charge your credit card, debit card, or checking account each month for the number of people you want to sponsor.

Remember, all donations are 100% tax deductible as Shelters By Jesus, Inc is a fully recognized non-profit association by the Internal Revenue Service. Shelters By Jesus, Inc. is a 501c3.